Woolwich and Dartford
TROLLEYBUSES

Robert J Harley

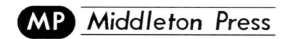

Middleton Press

First published November 1995

ISBN 1 873793 66 9

© Middleton Press 1995

Design - Deborah Goodridge

Published by Middleton Press
            Easebourne Lane
            Midhurst
            West Sussex
            GU29 9AZ
            Tel: 01730 813169
            Fax: 01730 812601

Printed & bound by Biddles Ltd,
            Guildford and Kings Lynn

CONTENTS

INTRODUCTION AND ACKNOWLEDGEMENTS

I have had great pleasure in assembling the pictures for this album. Many of the scenes which appear in the following pages have brought into focus a wealth of childhood memories. We often used to catch the trolley for family outings to Danson Park, and a regular Saturday morning trip to Bexleyheath Clock Tower enabled me to observe the fascinating spectacle of a seemingly endless procession of vehicles passing through or terminating at the Broadway. I recall clinging on for dear life as we accelerated out of Welling Corner..surely on no other form of public transport could one experience such "G" forces as the driver whisked the trolleybus away to the next stop! All this ended in 1959 when rather mundane diesel buses took over. Many locals now regret the passing of the silent, efficient and pollution free mode of transport which the trolleybuses offered. The following pictures only serve to remind us of the service that we have lost.

This journey into the past has been made possible by the photographers whose names appear in the text. I would like to thank C.Carter, B.T.Cooke, Alan Cross, B.J.Cross, John Gillham, Ken Glazier, Terry Russell, Lyndon Rowe, Don Thompson and Ann Watkins (for the loan of material from the collection of the late Alan Watkins). My gratitude also goes to Mrs S.Leitch for permission to use photographs from the late Dr H.Nicol. Much information has been gleaned from conversations with Allan Bedford, George Tapp, Richard Elliott, Ted Oakley and Peter Moore. I have consulted other books on the London trolleybus system by Ken Blacker, Michael Dryhurst, Keith Farrow and Hugh Taylor. A special word of thanks is necessary to John Smith of "Lens of Sutton" for all his help over the years.

Several views from the tramway era have been included in this book and the reader is directed to the companion Middleton Press albums, *Greenwich and Dartford Tramways* and *North Kent Tramways* for a selection of pre-trolleybus material. I have also used London Transport circulars extensively to document the early years of trolleybus operation. These staff notices show some of the problems encountered by this new form of transport and the solutions which were adopted. Finally, I have been unable to discover the identities of several of the photographers whose work features in this album; I tender my apologies to anyone whose name I have missed.

Trolleybus wiring diagram of the Woolwich to Dartford area.

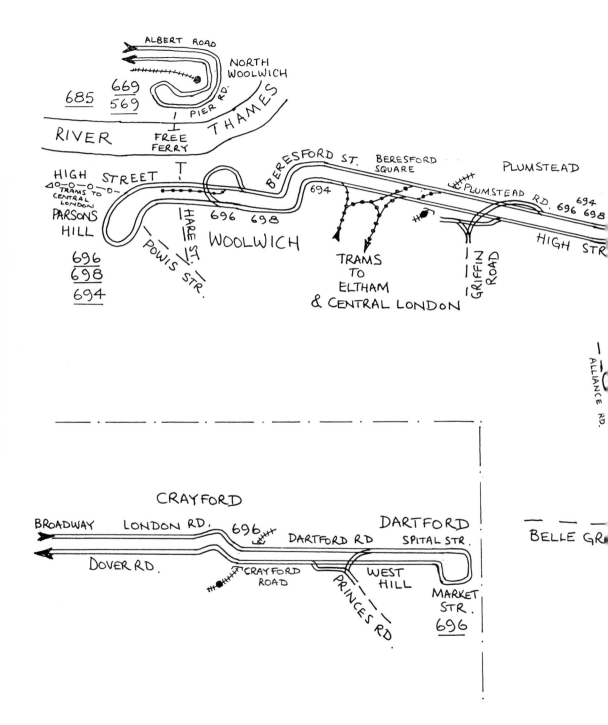

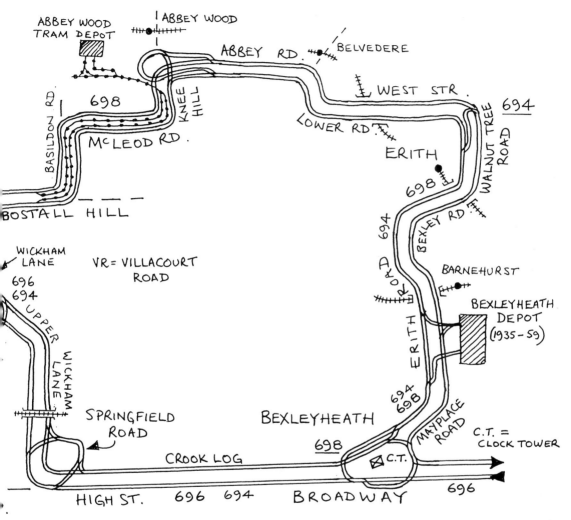

ABBEY WOOD
TRAM DEPOT

ABBEY WOOD

ABBEY RD.

BELVEDERE

WEST STR.

694

BASILDON RD.

698

KNEE HILL

McLEOD RD.

LOWER RD.

ERITH

698

WALNUT TREE ROAD

BOSTALL HILL

WICKHAM LANE

VR = VILLACOURT ROAD

694

BEXLEY RD.

696
694

UPPER WICKHAM LANE

BARNEHURST

ERITH ROAD

BEXLEYHEATH DEPOT (1935-59)

SPRINGFIELD ROAD

BEXLEYHEATH

694 698

MAYPLACE ROAD

698

C.T. = CLOCK TOWER

CROOK LOG

C.T.

HIGH ST.   696   694   BROADWAY   696

WELLING

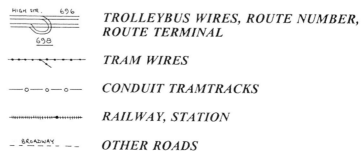

GEOGRAPHICAL SETTING

In trolleybus days the Woolwich area was administered by the London County Council; Bexley, Erith, Crayford and Dartford formed part of the county of Kent. The roads traversed by routes 696 and 698 varied in character from comparatively level Thamesside locations to the hills around Dartford and Wickham Lane in Welling.

HISTORICAL BACKGROUND

One of the first tasks confronting the new London Passenger Transport Board since its inception in 1933, was to improve transport facilities in the North Kent area. The local tramways were very run down and the decision was taken to replace them rather than to upgrade the track and modernise the rolling stock. The favoured substitute vehicle was the trolleybus and work was put in hand in the summer of 1935 to effect the conversion. Route 698 began operating from Woolwich to Bexleyheath on 10th November 1935. The direct service linking Woolwich, Welling, Bexleyheath, Crayford and Dartford opened on 24th November 1935 and was numbered 696. The fleet was housed in a new depot situated between Bexleyheath and Barnehurst.

These new transport facilities brought immediate benefits for the travelling public and passenger levels grew to such an extent that more trolleybuses were drafted in to cope. A further increase in traffic was occasioned by the Second World War. Workers needed transport to local factories engaged in producing armaments. Enemy action during the conflict caused the bombing of Bexley Depot in November 1940; the building also suffered a direct hit from a flying bomb on 29th June 1944. This resulted in severe damage to all the rolling stock and LT had to "borrow" vehicles from other depots to keep services going. The war also brought a reprieve for the rest of the London tramway system and shortly after the return of peace it was announced that the remaining trams would be replaced by motor buses. This change of policy meant that routes 696 and 698 stayed isolated from the main London trolleybus network. The last tram ran in July 1952.

An official announcement in 1954 sealed the fate of the trolleybuses, and London Transport began preparations for an enormous and costly changeover to diesel powered vehicles. Amongst the propaganda circulating at the time was a claim in the 1957 Annual Report of the British Transport Commission that.." (diesel) buses will prove a great deal more flexible and adaptable in service than the trolleybuses they are to replace.." The text continues in a similar vein, and it ends with a truly amazing statement..." medical research..showed that exhaust from a well maintained diesel engine constitutes no risk to health..." Thus the death warrant was signed and the day fixed for the execution was Tuesday, 3rd March 1959. Routes 696 and 698, together with Croydon service 654, were to form the first stage of the conversion scheme. On 4th March RT type buses began running in place of the electric vehicles, and shortly afterwards workmen commenced dismantling the overhead wires.

Extract from the LT timetable for December 1935

TROLLEYBUS SERVICES—continued

		MON. to FRI.		SATURDAY		SUNDA	
		First	Last	First	Last	First	La
696 WOOLWICH (Free Ferry) — DARTFORD (M. St) Via Plumstead, Wickham Lane, Welling, Bexleyheath, Crayford. Service interval 5-12 minutes. Journey time 45 mins. Through fare 8d.	Woolwich (Free Ferry) to Dartford (Market St.)	5 32	5 52 1049	5 32	5 52 1050	8 56	1048
	Woolwich (Free Ferry) to Bexleyheath	5 32	5 52 12 1	5 32	5 52 12 1	8 56	1142
	Welling to Dartford (Market Street)	5 52	6 12 11 9	5 52	6 12 1110	9 16	11 8
	Welling to Woolwich (Free Ferry)	5 8	5 28 1139	5 8	5 28 1139	8 33	1120
	Welling to Bexleyheath	5 52	6 12 1221	5 52	6 12 1221	9 16	12 2
	Bexleyheath to Woolwich (Free Ferry)	5 0	5 20 1131	5 0	5 20 1131	8 25	1112
	Bexleyheath to Dartford (Market Street)	5 0	5 24 1117	5 0	5 24 1118	8 55	1116
	Dartford (Market St.) to Woolwich(Free Ferry)	5 23	5 47 1114	5 23	5 47 1114	9 15	1055
	Dartford (Market St.) to Woolwich (Free Ferry)	5 23	5 47 1138	5 23	5 47 1138	9 15	1135
698 WOOLWICH (Free Ferry) — BEXLEYHEATH Via Abbey Wood, Belvedere, Erith, Northumberland Heath, Bexley Road. Service interval 6-12 mins. Journey time 43 mins. Through fare 7d.	Woolwich (Free Ferry) to Bexleyheath	6 3	6 10 1152	6 3	6 10 1152	9 46	115C
	Abbey Wood to Woolwich (Free Ferry)	5 46	5 54 1134	5 46	5 54 1134	9 28	113
	Abbey Wood to Bexleyheath	5 6	5 26 12 8	5 6	5 26 12 8	8 32	12 6
	Pier Road to Woolwich (Free Ferry)	5 32	5 40 1120	5 32	5 40 1120	9 14	111
	Pier Road to Woolwich (Free Ferry)	5 20	5 40 1222	5 20	5 40 1222	8 46	122C
	Bexley depot to Abbey Wood	4 40	5 0 1134	4 40	5 0 1134	8 6	1134
	Bexley depot to Woolwich (Free Ferry)	5 23	5 31 1111	5 23	5 31 1111	9 5	111C
	Bexleyheath to Woolwich (Free Ferry)	5 19	5 27 11 7	5 19	5 27 11 7	9 1	11 6
	Bexleyheath to Abbey Wood	5 19	5 27 1130	5 19	5 27 1130	9 1	1130

TRAM TO TROLLEYBUS

1. The first appearance of twin wire overhead in the area was in 1910 when the LCC Tramways opened the Beresford Square to Eltham Church route. The authorities at Greenwich Observatory would not permit a conventional single wire system with return of the current via the rails, so the arrangement pictured here was settled on. It survived until 1927. The positive and negative wires were 3ft./914mm apart; the later LT trolleybus standard wire spacing was 2ft./610mm. (R.J.Harley Coll.)

2. This view taken in Bexleyheath Broadway, neatly illustrates the "problem" facing London Transport in the early 1930s. This single track and loop layout was in dire need of renewal. It was traversed by four wheel trams which were only permitted to run at half power because of the state of the permanent way. No wonder the decision makers were swayed by the prospect of the trolleybus providing a modern, streamlined transport facility, more in tune with the "brave new world" they were endeavouring to achieve. (H.Nicol)

3.   Another concern was the cost of maintaining miles of worn tracks. LT had a statutory obligation to keep the surrounding roadway in good condition. This view shows a tram about to emerge into Dartford High Street by the triangular junction with Hythe Street. The rails leading to Lowfield Street in the left foreground carried the Wilmington service which was replaced by buses in 1934. The new 696 service would simplify the transport infrastructure here.   (H.Nicol)

4.   The first indication of the new order was the arrival of the tower wagons to erect the trolleybus overhead. This vehicle has been converted from a rather ancient Tilling bus and it still retains its solid tyres! The scene is near the Woolwich Arsenal gate at Beresford Square.   (H.Nicol)

5.   Here in Plumstead High Street work has begun on installing trolleybus overhead fittings. During the summer of 1935 the tram wires on the section from Woolwich to Abbey Wood were incorporated into the new layout. Dual tram/trolleybus working continued here until July 1952. (G.N.Southerden)

Extract from LT circular, October 1937

1598.—NOTICE TO DRIVERS.

Complaints have been received that Drivers of Trams and Trolleybuses are not exercising care in passing men cleaning overhead lamps.

Special care should be exercised when passing tower wagons when the men are at work.

6.   Above car 1468 is some of the temporary wiring employed in Bexleyheath Broadway for the transition period between the two forms of electric traction. Temporary wires also existed in Bexley Road, Erith where the tramtrack was offset to one side of the road. At Crook Log, Welling the width of the carriageway allowed the single track and loops tramway to be wired separately from the new trolleybus overhead.   (B.J.Cross Coll.)

7.   Accommodation had to be found for the trolleybuses, but unfortunately the old Bexley tram depot, as seen here, was deemed unsuitable for conversion. Space was limited on this site and the former Erith depot, which might have been a possibility, had already been disposed of. The only solution was to construct a brand new depot which could contain all the servicing facilities needed. (A.J.Watkins Coll.)

8. This view demonstrates the ample space available at the new depot. The building was sited in a predominantly residential area, and it was London's sole new, purpose built trolleybus depot. The only "fly in the ointment" was the attitude of the next door neighbours who forced LT to take drastic noise abatement measures to ensure that nocturnal vehicle movements were conducted quietly. (L.Rowe)

9. Once everything was in place, then publicity photos like this one would be distributed to local councils and newspaper editors. This line up of brand new vehicles is awaiting the call to service. They certainly look more attractive than their rail bound predecessors. (LT official photo)

Extract from LT circular, June 1936

1068.—NOISE.

Notice to Drivers and Conductors—Bexley Depot.

Complaints have been received of noise during the late evening and early morning.

Every effort must be made to avoid unnecessary noise and to give local residents as little cause for complaint as possible.

When leaving the depot the motor generator sets must not be started up until the vehicles are in service, and on arriving at the depot the motor generator sets must be shut down on reaching the forecourt. In both cases buses can be illuminated by the battery emergency lamps.

When taking a bus out of the depot or running in, all operations must be carried out as quietly as possible and special care taken to avoid slamming the cab door, unnecessarily sounding horn, shouting, etc.

PARSONS HILL, WOOLWICH TO BERESFORD SQUARE

10. Our journey by trolleybus begins at Parsons Hill, Woolwich where we observe a line of three trolleys headed by 766B. This vehicle had been rebodied by East Lancashire Coachbuilders after it had sustained war damage. The Bexley routes were well stocked with rebodied vehicles. (C.Carter)

11. The next arrival, 430C, sports a new body supplied by Northern Coachbuilders. The traction pole to the left of the trolley bears the marking C12; the standards used for the 1943 extension from Woolwich Ferry to Parsons Hill were all lettered with a C prefix. This narrow side street and much of the property hereabouts was swept away by John Wilson Street, the new dual carriageway approach road to the Woolwich Ferry.   (A.B.Cross)

12. The restricted space available at the terminus is readily apparent in this view looking north towards the Odeon Cinema. In the shadows stands a motorcycle and sidecar which once provided essential transport for many a small family. The advert on the back of 415 is a further sign that the private car was making inroads into passenger levels, however, in this February 1959 photo, the intensity of service on routes 696 and 698 was still impressive. (J.C.Gillham)

825.—NEW TROLLEYBUS SERVICE Nos. 696 and 698.

Notice to Inspectors and Conductors—Abbey Wood and Bexley Depots.

Commencing on Sunday, 10th November, 1935, Tramway Service No. 98 will be withdrawn and Trolleybus Service No. 698 will operate between Woolwich Free Ferry and Bexleyheath via Abbey Wood and Erith.

On the same date Tramway Service No. 40 will be curtailed at Beresford Square, but Service Nos. 36 and 38 will continue to operate to and from Abbey Wood.

At a date to be notified later Tramway Service No. 96 will be withdrawn and Trolleybus Service No. 696 will operate between Woolwich Free Ferry and Dartford (Market Street). The Tramway between Dartford and Horns Cross will be abandoned, but a 2d. Workman return fare will be obtainable between these points on the bus service. This should be made known to passengers.

Fares.

Ordinary fares between Bexleyheath and Abbey Wood and between Abbey Wood and Free Ferry will remain as at present, and fares overlapping Abbey Wood will be built up by the addition of the fares applying in each area.

Extract from LT circular, December 1935

13. We come in closer behind trolley 415, which was a Leyland vehicle constructed in 1936/7 with seats for 70 passengers. It was rebodied in 1945/6. The photographer is standing next to the railings which surrounded ornamental lawns and flower beds; this oasis of green has also now disappeared under a layer of concrete. (A.B.Cross)

14. A trolleybus approaches Parsons Hill after having set down its last passenger. Note that the front destination blind has already been turned to indicate a short working to Welling Corner. Behind trolley 472 is the rear wall of the Granada Cinema. (Lens of Sutton)

15. This is the last day of trams in London, 5th July 1952. To the right of car 560 is Hare Street which once served as the feeder road to the old Woolwich Ferry landing stage. In the background several trolleybuses, a tram and an RT diesel bus demonstrate the diversity of London's public transport at this period. Less than seven years after this scene was captured on film, electric street traction will have vanished totally from Woolwich. (R.J.Harley Coll.)

Extension of Trolleybus Routes 696 and 698

3234

On and after Wednesday, the 14th July, Routes 696 and 698 were extended from the Free Ferry to the new turning circle and stand in Parsons Hill.

1. Revised stopping places are in operation as follows :—

At Free Ferry

Eastbound: Trams to stop opposite Nos. 119/120 as at present.

Trolleybuses to stop at T.S. 5 outside the " Crown and Anchor " P.H.

Westbound: Trams to stop at T.S. 4 as at present. Trolleybuses to stop at T.S. 15 as at present.

At Powis Street

Eastbound: Trams to stop by request at the street lamp outside the A. and J. Garage, the stop outside the Enon Chapel will be abolished.

Trolleybuses to stop outside the Odeon Cinema in Parsons Hill.

Westbound: Trams to stop by request outside the doorway of No. 142, High Street. Trolleybuses proceeding into Parsons Hill to stop outside No. 192, Powis Street to set down only.

Extract from LT circular, July 1943

16. Near the Woolwich Ferry turning circle was situated the change pit where trams switched from overhead to the underground conduit method of current collection. In this part of Woolwich High Street there were several restaurants and tea shops, plus the Crown and Anchor for those who wished to imbibe something stronger. (C.Carter)

1138.—CYCLISTS.

Notice to Trolleybus Drivers.

Complaints have been received that owing to the silent running of the new trolleybuses cyclists are at times unaware that they are being overtaken.

Drivers should give due warning when overtaking.

Extract from LT circular, August 1936

17. The Kentish Independent was the local newspaper which informed people of the changeover to trolleybuses throughout 1935. Many of the reports harped on the luxurious qualities of the new vehicles. There is no doubt that the two trolleybuses seen here at the original Woolwich terminus, embodied in the public mind a style and comfort sadly lacking in the trams they replaced. This view dates from November 1935. (LT official photo)

833.—ROUTE Nos. 696 and 698.

The following maximum speeds must be strictly observed :—

30 Miles an hour.

In Dover Road and Dartford Road, between Bexley Council Offices and Devonshire Avenue, Dartford. In Park View Road, Bexley.

20 Miles an hour.

In High Street, Welling.
In Dartford between Devonshire Avenue and the turning loop.

10 Miles an hour.

While passing round the curve at Wickham Church, Wickham Lane, in the downhill direction.

Extract from LT circular, January 1936

18. Looking in the opposite direction to the previous photo, we observe trolley 114, a short wheelbase Leyland vehicle of 1935 which had seats for 60 people. London Transport has thoughtfully provided a passenger shelter and a stop sign which lists the important locations served by route 698. (LT official photo)

19. The date is February 1959 and the driver of this 698 slows to pass under the overhead frog leading to the old terminus at Woolwich Ferry. Excessive speed at junctions was one of the most common causes of dewirements. (L.Rowe)

20. Gaps in the housing at the corner of Beresford Street and Woolwich High Street were due to the demolition of war damaged properties. It was only in the fifties that the opportunity was taken to widen the road at this point. Note the new traction standards and wiring being installed to the right of the trolleybus. The granite setted roadway and the tramlines bear witness to a past era. (R.J.Harley Coll.)

21. We return to the same corner featured in the previous view. Car 1385 passes an H1 class Leyland in a classic street scene of 1948. A similar vehicle to the trolleybus pictured here, is preserved at the Paris Transport Museum. (B.T.Cooke)

22. At the eastern end of Beresford Street we encounter a brace of trolleys standing by the queueing pens which were positioned to cater for Arsenal workers, shoppers and bargain hunters visiting Woolwich Market. All of whom would line up in civilised British fashion to wait to board the next 696 or 698. (Lens of Sutton)

1382.—NEW TYPE STOP SIGN.

ABBEY WOOD TO BEXLEYHEATH VIA ERITH. WICKHAM LANE (PLUMSTEAD HIGH STREET) TO DARTFORD VIA WELLING.

On Wednesday, 7th April, 1937, the signs throughout the above-mentioned routes will be replaced by the new type of sign which reads "**Bus Stop,**" and is to be observed by trolleybuses and buses.

23. Tramcar 559 is making a valedictory appearance in Beresford Square and in a few hours, the only performer left on stage will be the trolleybus. Ironically, the tramtracks at this location outlived the trolleybuses. Vast road "improvements" have now affected this area, and although the former Woolwich Arsenal Gate has been preserved, the rest of the Square is but a mere shadow of its former self. (Lens of Sutton)

24. The tramlines have now been filled in, but the trolleybuses still bump over the granite setts. This picture conjures up a fine summer's day in the late 1950s. This is the heyday of small shops, black and white TV, the Light Programme, Hancock's Half Hour, Saturday morning films at the cinema, cheap fares and full employment!   (R.J.Harley Coll.)

25. The tram on service 46 is about to slip past one of the market stalls and turn into Woolwich New Road. The encroaching trolleybus seems to be offering rival advice as to the choice of alcoholic beverage! In the background, the Ordnance Arms and the Royal Mortar add to the feeling of well-being.   (B.T.Cooke)

26. Another photo taken in July 1952 shows 423 with the cab and passenger windows open on this warm summer's day. The location is Plumstead Road close to Beresford Square. (A.B.Cross)

PLUMSTEAD TO WICKHAM LANE

27. At Plumstead Station a trolleybus crests the bridge over the railway. Note that the wiring has been arranged to avoid placing traction standards on the bridge. One of the notices directs customers to Plumstead Goods Yard, whilst the other poster advertises cheap day returns to well known seaside resorts. This station is featured in Middleton Press album *Charing Cross to Dartford*. (L.Rowe)

28. On the eastern side of the railway bridge, rush hour is in full swing as a Dartford bound trolleybus leaves the stop ahead of an Abbey Wood bound 177 bus. Some of the wires leading to the Griffin Road reverser can be observed to the left of the trolley. (A.B.Cross)

Destination blinds issued to routes 696 and 698

PRIVATE
TO HIRE A BUS
APPLY 55 BROADWAY SW1
ABBEY 1234
PLUMSTEAD
STATION
WICKHAM LANE
VILLACOURT RD
WELLING CORNER
CRAYFORD
PRINCES ROAD
STATION ROAD
ERITH
DARTFORD MKT ST
VIA WELLING
& BEXLEYHEATH
WOOLWICH FERRY
VIA ERITH
& ABBEY WOOD
BEXLEYHEATH
MARKET PLACE
VIA WELLING
WORKMAN
DARTFORD MKT ST
VIA ERITH
& BEXLEYHEATH
DEPOT
ABBEY WOOD
PLUMSTEAD
WELLING
BEXLEYHEATH
CRAYFORD
696
WOOLWICH
PLUMSTEAD
WICKHAM LANE
WELLING CORNER
696
BEXLEYHEATH
CRAYFORD
WEST HILL
DARTFORD
PLUMSTEAD
ABBEY WOOD
ERITH
BARNEHURST
698
ERITH
NORTHUMBERLAND HTH
BARNEHURST
BEXLEYHEATH
EXTRA
696
698

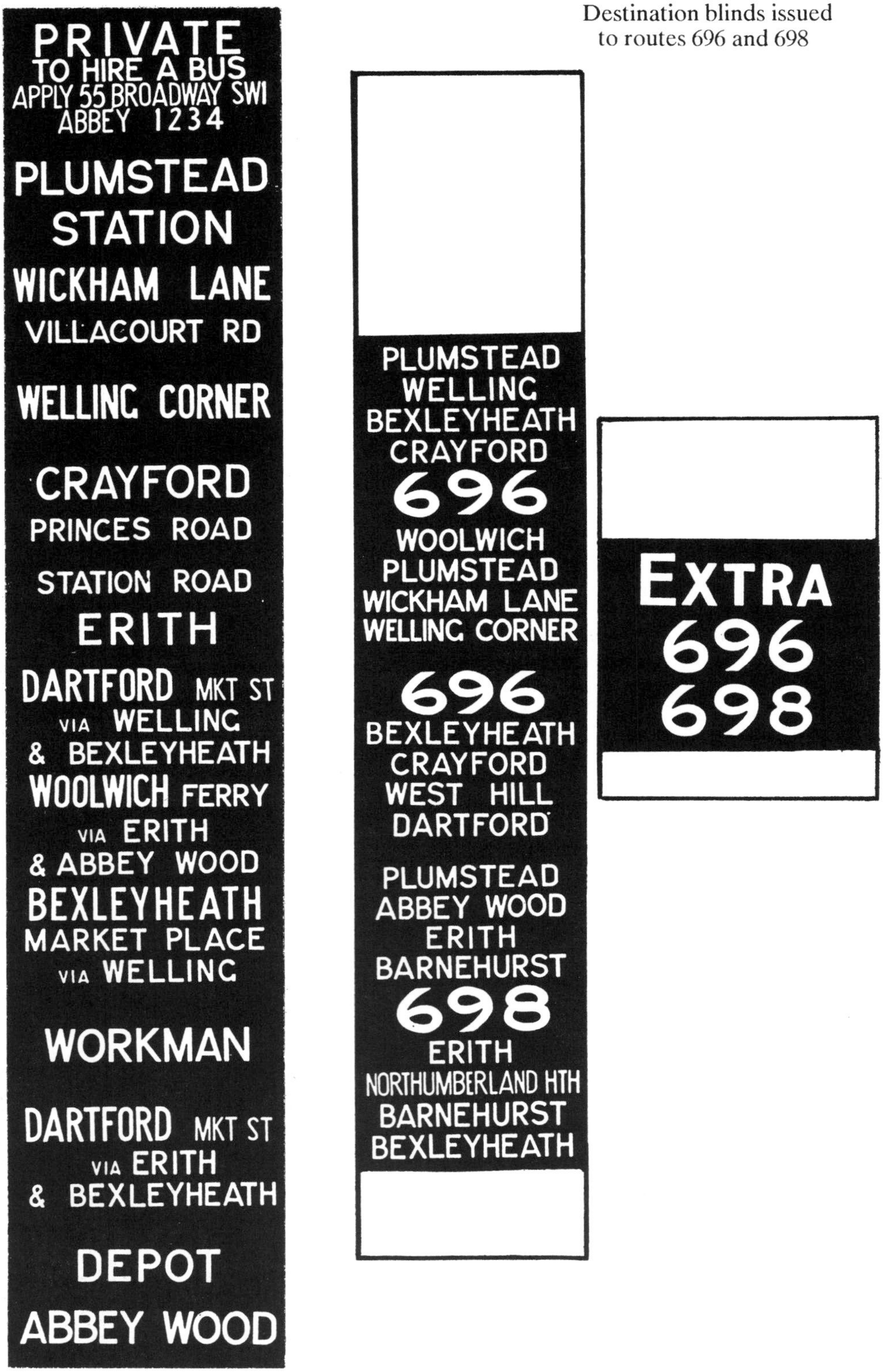

29. Trams and trolleybuses had to compete for road space along Plumstead High Street, and in this scene near Reidhaven Road, the 36 tram is about to tackle the single track. The trolleybus behind will have to be patient, since its rail bound sister is using the positive wire of the trolleybus overhead, therefore no overtaking was possible! (J.C.Gillham)

30. Another scene from Plumstead High Street illustrates the restricted width of this main thoroughfare. The view is dated 28th June 1952. (J.C.Gillham)

31. The right hand pavement is crowded with shoppers as we near the junction with Lakedale Road. As can be seen, there was a frequent tram and trolleybus service in these parts and all the public transport vehicles on display are pollution free. (J.C.Gillham)

32. The parting of the ways for routes 696 and 698 occurred at the eastern end of Plumstead High Street. The driver of the 696 puts out his hand to indicate he is about to turn into Wickham Lane. He also glances at the hooded junction indicator box affixed to the traction standard by Camrose Street. This device showed that the trolley booms had taken the correct wires.   (D.A.Thompson)

33. Most drivers were skilled and they would avoid clipping the traffic island at the entrance to Wickham Lane with their back tyres. In wartime it was particularly important to save rubber as the LT circular indicates.   (T.M.Russell)

Where there's a Wheel—

There's a way of lengthening its life and beating the rubber shortage.

A new task, an urgent task, and it's the privilege of all our bus and trolleybus drivers to share in it straightaway.

They can help in its accomplishment by preventing unnecessary wear and tear.

34. Trolley 430C is about to leave Wickham Lane and rejoin the 698 wires in Plumstead High Street. On the side of the trolleybus is an advert for Mitchells of Erith. This well loved local store has also been a casualty of so called progress, and it closed its doors in 1960. (C.Carter)

LAST TROLLEY TO VILLACOURT ROAD

35. In the final hours of trolleybus operation, photographer Alan Cross charted the progress of 410 as it made the only scheduled turn of the day in Villacourt Road. Here it is seen in Wickham Lane with the conductor about to leap off the rear platform to change the pull frog for Villacourt Road. (A.B.Cross)

37. The turning circle was at the junction of Villacourt Road and Alliance Road. It was constructed by LT in the autumn of 1940 as an emergency turnback to counteract disruption to services caused by bombing. It is doubtful whether this facility in the middle of a sleepy, suburban housing estate would have been sanctioned in peacetime. Most local residents were not trolleybus enthusiasts. (J.C.Gillham)

36. The conductor has now crossed Wickham Lane and he waits at the entrance to Villacourt Road. He carries on his front a Gibson ticket machine, which was introduced on routes 696/698 in July 1954. It replaced the old Bell Punch method. Crews attached to Bexleyheath Depot used to refer to the two routes as the "sixes" and the "eights". (A.B.Cross)

| Bexley Depot | | 2548 |

Notice to Inspectors and Conductors

A new numbered ticket will be put into use for $1\frac{1}{2}$d. and 2d. ordinary single and 1d. child values as existing supplies are exhausted. Specimens are exhibited in the depot. The stage point numbers remain unaltered except for the following :—

Fare Stage Point	New No.	Remarks
Bexleyheath Depot	37	Previously unnumbered
Wheatley Arms ..	33	These numbers apply only on Route No. 694. The present numbers are retained for use on Route No. 698.
Carlton Road ..	32	
Brook Street ..	31	
Barnehurst Bridge	30	

Farebills will be revised to shew the new numbers.

Extract from LT circular, August 1940

38. Parts of the wiring along Villacourt Road were supported by these stylish bowstring bracket arms. They were designed by LT as part of an attempt to minimise the alleged unsightly aspect of trolleybus overhead. Credit for their final shape seems to lie with Lionel Harvey, the former Ilford Tramways Manager, and Charles Holden, who was one of the leading lights in the team assembled by Frank Pick to enhance the house image of the new London Passenger Transport Board. (A.B.Cross)

40. We take a final glance at the wiring leading to Villacourt Road. In the distance past the motor bus is the entrance to Plumstead Bus Garage by Kings Highway. This garage was closed in 1981 and it has subsequently been demolished. (D.A.Thompson)

39. A chapter closes and 410 writes finis for this little known backwater of the huge London trolleybus sytem. (A.B.Cross)

WELLING

41. We now enter the county of Kent in company with B2 class, number 98; this trolley was later severely damaged in a flying bomb attack on Bexley Depot in June 1944. It returned to service, rebuilt by Northern Coachbuilders as a fully fledged long wheelbase vehicle, reclassified D2C. All this was in the future when this publicity shot was taken in November 1935. (LT official photo)

42. A little more than 23 years after the previous photo we encounter trolley 98 again as it tackles the grade at the corner of Okehampton Crescent and Upper Wickham Lane. The electric trolleybuses coped very well with hills and they could outpace their internal combustion engined rivals. (L.Rowe)

43. The Welling to Bexleyheath railway crosses Upper Wickham Lane just short of the main shopping area of Welling. There is elaborate troughing under the bridge to carry the overhead wires, and the adjacent shuttering is fixed so as to prevent wayward trolley poles from striking the metal girders of the bridge. (D.A.Thompson)

44. The wires to the right lead to Springfield Road and were used for short workings to Welling Corner. The only electric traction on view is the dark blue and cream, Express Dairies milk float. This scene, devoid of trolleybuses, recalls the 1958 bus strike which lasted from 5th May to 21st June. During this period the author remembers passing by train over the railway bridge in the background and looking out at the rain dripping off the lifeless trolleybus wires. When the 696s and 698s returned, there was much sparking from the trolley heads as they coped with the debris of many weeks inactivity. (J.C.Gillham)

45. Welling Corner on a dull day late in February 1959 sees a 696 turning into the High Street. A string of small lights was positioned between the up and down wires and these were illuminated in foggy weather or when visibility was poor, so that drivers did not miss the bend and go careering on up Belle Grove Road in the direction of Shooters Hill! (L.Rowe)

46. This picture is taken looking east along Welling High Street. Note the Timothy Whites store which was part of a chain later absorbed by Boots the Chemists. The car at the end of the queue behind the trolleybus is an American Oldsmobile. This vehicle would have probably been equipped with a radio, in which case the reception would have been marred by crackling interference from the overhead wires. (C.Carter)

---

696 | .   **Dartford - Welling - Plumstead - Woolwich**   P.M. times are in heavy figures

Via Spital Street (return via Market Place and High St.), West Hill, Dartford Road, Crayford Road, Bexleyheath Broadway, Crook Log, Park View Road, Welling High Street, Upper Wickham Lane, Wickham Lane, Plumstead High Street, Plumstead Road, Beresford Square, Beresford Street, Woolwich High Street.

RAILWAY STATIONS SERVED : Dartford, Crayford, Welling, Plumstead, Woolwich Arsenal

Service interval: WEEKDAYS, Dartford-Bexleyheath 4-5 mins. (Mon. to Fri. eve. 8 mins., Sat. eve. 6 mins.), Bexleyheath-Welling 4 mins. (peak hours 2½ mins., Mon. to Fri. eve. 8 mins., Sat. eve. 6 mins.); Welling-Woolwich 4 mins. (peak hours 2 mins., Mon. to Fri. eve. 8 mins., Sat. eve. 6 mins.); SUNDAY, Dartford-Bexleyheath 4 mins. (evening 8 mins.), Bexleyheath-Woolwich 4 mins.

	WEEKDAYS First	SUN. First	DAILY Last			WEEKDAYS First	SUN. First	DAILY Last
DARTFORD *Market Street*	....	5 23	....	6 6	9 49	10 19	11 12	WOOLWICH *Powis Street*
Bexleyheath *Market Place*	5 0	5 41	5 0	6 24	10 7	10 37	11 30	Welling Corner
Welling Corner	5 9	5 50	5 9	6 33	10 16	10 46	....	Bexleyheath *Market Place*
WOOLWICH *Powis Street*	5 28	6 11	5 30	6 54	10 37			DARTFORD *Market Street*

SPECIAL EARLY JOURNEYS—WEEKDAYS

Bexleyheath *Market Place* to Abbey Wood at 4 57 a.m. | Abbey Wood to Bexleyheath *Market Place* at 5 26 a.m.

Extract from LT timetable, December 1943

47. This is the stop by the Embassy Ballroom and many a traveller attired in a posh frock or a smart suit has alighted here to enjoy a good night out. Pasted on the traction standards are the dreaded official yellow notices stating that from 4th March 1959 trolleybus route 696 will be replaced by new bus route 96. (A.B.Cross)

48. The Springfield Road wires made an exit via Nags Head Lane seen on the right of the picture. A Dennis lorry is making a delivery to the nearby hostelry whilst the quiet, efficient trolleybus service proceeds as normal. (D.A.Thompson)

49. Park View Road, Welling lies along the northern boundary of Danson Park. In years gone by, many thousands were transported by the trolleybuses to events staged in the park. In post-war years the family budget could usually stretch to afford the hire of a rowing boat on the lake and then perhaps a return ticket on the steam miniature railway which ran by the water's side. (LT official photo)

CROOK LOG TO BEXLEYHEATH BROADWAY

50. Long before the present day swimming baths and traffic roundabout were constructed, a trolleybus pauses opposite the Crook Log Inn. On the outside this building still retains some of its "Olde Worlde" Kentish charm, but the days when drovers guided flocks of sheep past the front door to market in London, belonged to the distant past. (L.Rowe)

51. Bexleyheath Broadway is built on the old Dover Road, formerly the Roman Watling Street. This picture was taken by the Clock Tower in the early years of the trolleybus service. It shows Leyland D1, number 384, which was the only member of its class.
(Leyland Motors official photo)

52. The same spot as the previous view, but now time has shifted to the 1950s. The wiring layout has now been altered so that Dartford bound trolleys work one way round the Clock Tower in tandem with Erith bound 698s. The trolleybus in the centre of the picture is on route 698 and is turning into Market Place and thence into Mayplace Road West. (C.Carter)

53. The author used to spent many a happy hour watching this scene from his vantage point outside Lloyds Bank. Since those halcyon days of the fifties, the dire trend of town centre redevelopment has afflicted this location. Through traffic now uses no less than two by-pass highways and many of the shops have been flattened to be reborn as a hideous shopping mall. (A.Bedford Coll.)

54. Hide's of Bexleyheath are engaged in one of their periodic shop rebuilds, this time an extension is being constructed to house the new food hall. The era of supermarket shopping is at hand! On the transport front, the leading trolleybus displays an LT "fill in" poster either side of the front indicator box. These were used to avoid blank spaces occasioned by the lack of paid advertising. (Lens of Sutton)

55. The Clock Tower shows 3.30pm as trolley 799B passes along the one way section. The traction standard on the left survived for many years as a support pole for a street lamp. Latterly it was painted in Bexley London Borough light blue livery rather than the austere LT dark green. (C.Carter)

56. It is a tight squeeze for trolley 472 as it negotiates the bend on the eastern side of Market Place. For a few yards this 696 will share a common set of wires with route 698 before it branches off in the direction of Dartford. (D.A.Thompson)

57. Even in 1959 it seems that the economic climate could not sustain the Royal Arsenal Cooperative Society's radio and television shop. The trolleybus in the picture wasn't long for this world either and in two days RT buses on route 96 would be wafting diesel fumes over anyone standing on the pavement. (L.Rowe)

58. A photogenic location along the route was here at Shenstone Park where one of the original fleet of short wheelbase trolleybuses is captured on film in 1936. Osborne's, the furniture store in Bexleyheath Market Place, is offering a complete bedroom suite in walnut for just under £12. This was at a time when a new Ayling built house in Crayford could be purchased for a deposit of one pound and a weekly mortgage repayment of thirteen shillings and ninepence (68p)! For the sake of comparison, a trolleybus driver would have earned around four pounds eleven shillings (£4.55) for a 48 hour week. (LT official photo)

59. It is surprising that even in the 1950s there was not that much traffic about as we can see here by Shenstone Park as trolley 410 speeds along London Road. (D.A.Thompson)

60. The centre of Crayford contained a number of important industrial establishments many of whose workers arrived and departed by trolleybus. The public transport needs of the Crayford citizen were also served by several LT country bus routes and the Green Line coaches on routes 701 and 702. (L.Rowe)

61. The trolley on the left has just used the Princes Road reverser, which was constructed in 1942, and it is now waiting to take employees from the nearby Vickers Works. Note that the vehicle is rostered on a route 698 special working to Erith.   (D.A.Thompson)

2434 **Crayford Town Hall— Route 696.**

Drivers are instructed to exercise caution when passing Timpsons' Garage, just west of Crayford Town Hall. This is now a depot for A.R.P. ambulances and Fire Appliances which may suddenly emerge from the two bays furthest from the Town Hall.

Extract from LT circular, March 1940

62. Raising the overhead with their trolley booms, these three vehicles wait for homeward bound workers. Just before 5pm each weekday evening, six trolleybuses would reverse here at approximately one minute intervals. This rather poignant scene was taken on the very last day of trolleybus operation. The Morris Minor has just crossed the boundary from Dartford into Crayford. After 1965 this became the county boundary between Kent and London. (J.C.Gillham)

63. The process of reversing across Crayford Road and into Princes Road was conducted in an age before streams of motor traffic. Although even then, it was an awkward manoeuvre and matters would have been improved by installing a turning circle instead. Interestingly, the modern road layout at this point features a roundabout. (LTPS)

64. This 696 descends West Hill, Dartford on the final leg of its eight mile journey from Woolwich. In 1958 the through adult fare was one shilling and sixpence (7p). (D.A.Thompson)

66. This location in the High Street by the Royal Victoria and Bull Hotel has already been captured on film in picture 3. This trolleybus view dates from 11th January 1959 and shows 407 slowing for the T junction with Lowfield Street. This area of Dartford is now a pedestrian precinct. (L.Rowe)

65. Trolley 473 makes its way through an animated scene in Spital Street, Dartford. A sister vehicle swings out to pass an obstruction in the left background by the junction with Hythe Street. In the 1960s/70s a new ring road system was built to take traffic away from Dartford town centre. (C.Carter)

67. From the look of the queue on the right, it would seem that the Country Bus Department is making its customers wait. The sole representative of the Central (red) Bus Department is above all this as it glides silently from High Street into Market Street. Unfortunately for those people waiting at the stop, LT turned down the idea of extending the trolleys to Gravesend. The proposed route was surveyed in about 1941/2, but nothing came of it. (C.Carter)

68. The front blind on 468 has been altered to show a special working 698 to Abbey Wood. This section of Market Street now forms part of the Dartford inner ring road. (Lens of Sutton)

69. Yet another short working vehicle is pictured at Dartford terminus. It occupies a space outside the marvellously named C.Haydn Chudleigh's Restaurant just in advance of the official stand outside the museum building. The driver of BPC 4 seems to be unaware of the one way rules governing this thoroughfare. (D.A.Thompson)

70. The original terminus in Market Street was wired for anti clockwise operation and the trolleybus seen here is using this wiring before it was altered in August 1952. The conductor has changed the blinds to show route 694; this former service number was used in the early post war years to indicate a short working, in this case to Station Road, Erith. Route 694 operated officially in the period May 1937 to January 1940; normally it ran on Sundays and Bank Holidays between Woolwich and Erith via Welling and Bexleyheath. It resumed a fitful existence for the summers of 1940-44 and finally ceased in May 1944. (Lens of Sutton)

Yc 8948

C Bx   L.T. Trolleybuses

Ch'nge Bexley Heath
(Market Place)   37

18		36
19	696	35
20	698	34
21		33
22		32
23	For conditions see Back	31
24		80
25	1½d., 2d. 3d 4d 5d 6d, 7d 1d Child	29
26		29
27		28

71. Several transport enthusiasts greet the arrival of DGY 474 as it pulls up behind another trolleybus at the terminus. (A.B.Cross)

Dartford Trolleybus Terminus 3257

The stop sign at this terminus will shortly be transferred from T.S. 882 to a position about 7 ft. east of the entrance to Messrs. Penney, Son and Parker's yard.

When the first bus is in position with the platform at the queue sign, the next bus must pull up in such a position that the entrance to the yard is kept clear.

1450.—NEW TROLLEYBUS ROUTE—WOOLWICH—ERITH VIA WELLING.

Notice to Inspectors and Conductors—Bexley Depot.

Commencing on Sunday, 16th May, 1937, a new trolley bus route (No. 694) will operate on Sundays only between Woolwich Free Ferry and Erith, " Wheatley Arms," via Welling and Bexleyheath.

Fares overlapping Bexleyheath Market Place will be as follows :—

Erith, " Wheatley Arms," &	d.	Carlton Road &	d.
Brook Street ...	1	Barnehurst Bridge	1
Barnehurst Bridge	1½	Bexleyheath Market Place ...	1½
Bexleyheath Market Place	2	Lion Road	2
Lion Road	2½	Brampton Road	2½
Brampton Road	3	" Guy, Earl of Warwick "... ...	3
" Guy, Earl of Warwick "	3½	Welling Corner	3½
Welling Corner	4	Lovel Avenue	4
Lovel Avenue	4½	" Foresters Arms," Wickham Lane	4½
" Foresters Arms," Wickham Lane	5	King's Highway	5
King's Highway	5½	" Plume of Feathers," Plumstead...	5½
" Plume of Feathers," Plumstead ...	6	Plumstead Station	6
Plumstead Station	6½	Beresford Square	6½
Beresford Square	7	Woolwich Free Ferry	7
Woolwich Free Ferry	7½		
Brook Street &		**Barnehurst Bridge &**	
Bexleyheath Market Place	1	Lion Road	1
Brampton Road	2	" Guy, Earl of Warwick "... ...	2
Welling Corner	3	Lovel Avenue	3
" Foresters Arms," Wickham Lane	4	King's Highway	4
" Plume of Feathers," Plumstead ...	5	Plumstead Station	5
Beresford Square	6	Woolwich Free Ferry	6

The new route number and destination wording " Erith via Welling and Bexleyheath " will be added to the destination blinds, but until these additions have been made blinds must be set as follows :—

(a) **Number Blind**—Shew 696.

(b) **Destination Blind**—On leaving Woolwich Free Ferry shew " Bexleyheath Market Place via Welling."
    On arrival at Welling Corner (when working to Erith) shew " Erith Station Road."
    On leaving Erith for Woolwich shew " Woolwich Ferry via Bexleyheath and Welling."

(c) **Sideblind**—Shew :—Woolwich.
        Plumstead.
        Wickham Lane.
        Welling.
        Bexleyheath.

72. The 696 bus stop is numbered as an guide to passengers unfamiliar with the street layout and the stopping arrangements of the numerous other local routes. A map of the numbered stops was displayed behind a glass panel fixed to each stop in the area. The peak hour service was around 19 vehicles an hour and the stand time allowed for each of these trolleybuses was around five minutes. (C.Carter)

1791.—DARTFORD—MARKET PLACE.

Drivers are instructed to exercise care when leaving the terminus and emerging on to the main road.

Extract from LT circular, April 1938

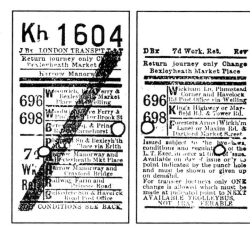

73. Trolley 808B heads away from the terminus towards Dartford High Street. On the left of the picture is the site of the pre-1952 terminus with a lone traction pole still standing.   (L.Rowe)

74. We encounter route 698 again as we witness a trolleybus pursued by an RT diesel bus leaving Plumstead High Street. Both vehicles depicted here are advertising the London Transport "Hop On A Bus" campaign which was launched on 5th November 1958. It was intended to boost ridership at a time when public confidence in LT had been severely dented by the long bus strike. (L.Rowe)

76. A novel feature of the route from Plumstead to Abbey Wood was the use of several of these gas lit stop signs which were illuminated at night. (C.Carter)

Uh 2133
(F Bx) LONDON TRANSPORT
9d WORKMAN RET.
Return journey only
Ch Bexleyheath Market Place
Harrow Manorway

| 696 | **W** Woolwich (Powis St.) Bexleyheath Market Place via Erith |
| 698 | |

W Woolwich (Powis St.) and Tower Rd. via Welling

B Beresford Sq. and Dartford Market Street via Welling

**For conditions see back

W Wickham Lane & Havelock Rd. Post Office via Erith

B Basildon Road McLeod Rd. and Tower Road via Erith

H Harrow Manorway and Dartford Market Street via Erith

BM 4889
O Bx   L.T. Trolleybuses

Ch'nge Bexley Heath (Market Place)	3′.
18	36
19	35
20	34
21	33
22	32
23	31
24	30
25	29
26	28
27	

696 698

For conditions see back

1½d., 2d. 3d. 4d. 5d. 7d Child.

75. Looking along Bostall Hill in April 1952, we catch sight of a 698 weaving its way past a stationary tramcar at Woodhurst Road loop and a parked car opposite the pre-fabs. (J.C.Gillham)

77. This view demonstrates very clearly the three wire overhead in Mc.Leod Road. It was possible on this stretch of road for a trolleybus to overtake a tram and vice versa. (Lens of Sutton)

78. The photographer is standing on the corner of Mc.Leod Road and Knee Hill, Abbey Wood. When trolleybus route 698 was inaugurated in 1935 it provided a useful through service from Erith to Woolwich. The tram service it replaced only ran as far as the Harrow Inn in the background. (D.A.Thompson)

79. The local postcard sellers were quick off the mark when it came to recording the latest transport innovation. The trolleybus to the right of the open fronted tram is pictured in a brand new state with its polished panels gleaming. However, the publisher thought he would play safe and the card was labelled "Tram Terminus, Abbey Wood." (B.J.Cross Coll.)

80. The tramtrack in the right foreground connects with Abbey Wood Depot in Abbey Wood Road. The LCC Tramways ended here at what was once the county boundary between Kent and London. Just next to the 698 trolleybus are the remains of tram rails laid by LT to provide a link to the former Erith system, these can be seen better in picture 110.   (J.C.Gillham)

ROUTE **698**		**Bexleyheath - Erith - Abbey Wood - Woolwich'**		P.M. times are in heavy figures

Via May Place Road West, Erith Road, Bexley Road, Walnut Tree Road, West Street, New Bridge, Lower Road, Picardy Street, Gilbert Road, Abbey Road, Knee Hill, McLeod Road, Basildon Road, Plumstead High Street, Plumstead Road, Beresford Square, Beresford Street, Woolwich High Street

RAILWAY STATIONS SERVED : Barnehurst, Erith, Belvedere, Abbey Wood, Plumstead, Woolwich Arsenal

Service interval : 5-6 minutes (evening 10 minute4).   Additional service, Saturday afternoon between Bexleyheath and Erith every 12 minutes.

	WEEKDAYS						SUNDAY				DAILY									
	*	First					First				Last									
BEXLEYHEATH *Market Place*....	4 37	5 9	....	...	....		5 18	...	...	...	9 31	10 9			...	....	...			
Erith *Wheatley Arms*...........	4 50	5 22	..	...	....		5 32	..	..	..	9 45	10 23			....	....				
Abbey Wood *Harrow Arms*........	5 4	5 36	..	...	...		5 47	..	..	..	10 0	10 38			....	....	...			
WOOLWICH *Powis Street*	..	5 52		..			6 3	..			10 16	..								
	*																			
WOOLWICH *Powis Street*	....			5 42	...			6 6			10 20									
Abbey Wood *Harrow Arms*......	5 6	5 46	5 58	..			6 2	6 32	..	..	10 36	10 45			...	....				
Erith *Wheatley Arms*.........	5 20	6 1	6 13	..			6 17	6 37	..	..	10 51	11 0			....	....				
BEXLEYHEATH *Market Place*..	5 33	6 15	6 27	..			6 21	6 51	..	..	11 5	11 14			*-Early journey					

SPECIAL JOURNEYS

Bexleyheath to Woolwich, via Welling, WEEKDAYS at 5 10 a.m. : SUNDAY at 6 58 a.m.
Dartford to Woolwich, SUNDAY at 7 27 a.m.
Woolwich to Dartford, SUNDAY at 6 21 a.m.

Extract from LT timetable, December 1943

81. A splendid shot of 432 as it turns into Knee Hill from Abbey Road...this was in the days before the Manor Way flyover and the Thamesmead estate. (D.A.Thompson)

82. After the flying bomb disaster of June 1944, there was a massive influx of "foreign" vehicles to cover Bexley's losses. FXH 549 is an M1 class AEC of 1940 and it has been drafted in from East London. Note the wartime masked headlamps, white painted mudguards, windows with blast netting and the poster on the side urging more women to join LT as conductors. (A.Bedford Coll.)

BELVEDERE TO ERITH

83. Picardy Street by Belvedere Station is traversed by 471. On the left of the picture, a driver and a conductor wait for the next eastbound trolley. The whole highway here was later realigned to a position south of the original road. Strangely, some of the old traction poles managed to survive this destruction and they stood for many years in front of a new parade of shops. (D.A.Thompson)

84. Much road replanning has changed the nature of this location since the departure of the trolleybuses from Belvedere. Note the rather ornate RACS building in the background and the clutch of small, friendly shops to the right. (C.Carter)

85. The pub on the hillside stands at the corner of Picardy Road. It is one of the few landmarks still recognisable today. Trolley 444 is in the old Station Road and the driver will shortly turn to his left into Picardy Street. (C.Carter)

86. The bridge over the Belvedere to Erith railway line is still known as New Bridge in memory of its construction by Erith Council in 1904/5 to carry the new electric tramways. (L.Rowe)

87. St.John's Church, Erith is steeped in history and can trace the names of its incumbents back to 1331. Here it offers a spendid Kentish setting for this study of a 698 about to turn into West Street. Above the trolleybus is a string of "fairy lights" similar to the set which existed at Welling Corner. This photo exudes an atmosphere totally different from the hustle and bustle of some of the inner London trolleybus termini. (L.Rowe)

88. Tramlines still mark the curve from West Street to Walnut Tree Road in this February 1953 picture. The trolleybus is parked with its trolley booms stowed under the retaining hooks at the rear of the vehicle. On the right hand side of the road is the old open air swimming pool. (J.C.Gillham)

89. We now set our sights towards the River Thames; in the distance a ship navigates downstream. This was at a time when much of the nation's commerce was still reliant on the shipping trade. In the foreground is the trolleybus turning circle at the end of Walnut Tree Road. On the right, the former Cannon and Gaze flour mill looms large on the river bank. (D.A.Thompson)

90. Framed by trees is the old Erith tram depot which was sold by LT in December 1933. The road along which the trolleybus is travelling was specially constructed for Erith Council Tramways in the first decade of the twentieth century.   (C.Carter)

91. As the mist rolls in from the Thames, this 698 pauses at the stop in Walnut Tree Road which was convenient for the nearby Erith Library.   (L.Rowe)

92. Trolley 395B shows EXTRA on the route number blind, and it is obviously rostered to augment the service from Erith to Bexleyheath Broadway. The new LT bus stop is an ominous sign; many of these were erected just before the conversion to diesel buses. The old stop signs had been removed because they were attached to traction standards which would be uprooted after trolleybus operation ceased. (C.Carter)

1672.—LOOKING OUT FOR PASSENGERS.

Notice to Trolleybus Drivers and Conductors—Route No. 698.

Drivers and Conductors are instructed to keep a sharp look-out for passengers transferring from Central Bus Route No. 99 to Trolleybus Route No. 698 at trolleybus stopping place west of Victoria Road Railway Bridge, Erith.

Extract from LT circular, December 1937

93. Much of Erith has been redeveloped since this photo was taken at the Wheatley Hotel. A completely new road scheme has changed the character of the town centre and a roundabout now exists at the junction depicted here. (A.Bedford Coll.)

94. Southern Region suburban trains provided competition for the trolleybuses. Trolley 431 passes the station direction board by the entrance to Victoria Road. (C.Carter)

NORTHUMBERLAND HEATH TO
BEXLEYHEATH BROADWAY

95. A small local shopping centre had grown up at Northumberland Heath on the road from Erith to Bexleyheath. Trolleybuses seem to have been rarely photographed at this spot, so we are particularly fortunate to catch a glimpse of 434 as it stands outside the Northumberland Heath branch of the Westminster Bank. (Lens of Sutton)

96. We now leave the area of the former Erith Council Tramways and arrive at Courtleet Parade in Bexley territory. Milestone's Garage in the centre of the picture was once well known as the local Jowett and Bradford motor agent. (D.A.Thompson)

97. A trolleybus ascends the hill into Barnehurst with Bursted Wood on the left. As can be seen, there was a distinct rural feel to parts of routes 696 and 698. (L.Rowe)

98. The depot in Erith Road is passed by one of its inmates. Note the diesel buses on route 122 which terminated on the depot forecourt. This sensible use of LT property by the bus department began on 9th September 1936, almost a year after the full commissioning of the depot. A set of wires circled the building and many apocryphal stories are told about unofficial holders of the circuit "lap record"! (C.Carter)

99. Members of the official party wait outside the depot for the ceremonial first run of route 698 in November 1935. The original name for the building was Bexley Depot, but by the end of trolleybus operations in 1959, the official title was Bexleyheath Depot. Note that the bases of the traction standards on the depot forecourt have been protected by a concrete "collar" to lessen the potential damage to the overhead which could be caused vehicles colliding with the pole. (C.F.Klapper Coll.)

100. Inside the depot, seemingly ostracised by all her longer wheelbase sisters, is one of the remaining "short" vehicles: B2 class Leyland, number 104. The official capacity of the depot was 75 vehicles, although no less than 84 trolleys were crammed in at the time of the infamous flying bomb attack. The depot was allocated the code letters BX in 1950, and it became Bexleyheath Garage on 4th March 1959. Since then it has had a chequered history, being closed and reopened as part of successive reorganisations of the local bus services.   (D.Trevor Rowe)

101. Mayplace Road West leads to Bexleyheath Market Place and this 698 is caught on film just after it has coasted under the section feed. Power was supplied to the overhead at roughly half mile intervals. The driver is slowing for the one way trip round the Clock Tower and within a few yards this vehicle will rejoin route 696 wires.
(A.Bedford Coll.)

102. We reach the end of our nostalgic journey by trolleybus routes 696 and 698 here at Bexleyheath Clock Tower. An H1 class Leyland, built in 1938, heads out on a short working to Abbey Wood.   (D.A.Thompson)

103. Because of an historical anomaly, several tracts of land north of the Thames passed to the Metropolitan Borough of Woolwich in 1889. Trolleybuses first arrived here on Sunday, 6th February 1938 and the section of route from Canning Town was the longest extension opened by LT over previously tramless roads. Here at North Woolwich two trolleybuses are depicted on the turning circle opposite the Free Ferry landing stage. The round structure on the left contains the lift and staircase which descend to the foot tunnel under the Thames. (J.H.Meredith)

104. Routes serving North Woolwich were the 685, 569 and 669, although only the latter service operated all day. The trolleybus in this picture has almost reached North Woolwich Station in Pier Road. The blinds show peak hour route 569 to Aldgate. Note the bus on route 101 which links North Woolwich with East Ham and Manor Park. Part of the 101 covered the former tramway from Royal Albert Docks to Wanstead Park; this is described in Middleton Press volume *East Ham and West Ham Tramways*. (C.Carter)

1710.—EXTENSION OF ROUTE 669 TO NORTH WOOLWICH (FREE FERRY).

Notice to Inspectors and Conductors—West Ham Depot.

On Sunday, 6th February, 1938, Route 669 was extended to operate between Stratford Broadway and North Wool-wich (Free Ferry).

TICKETS.

Tickets containing the necessary sections for use on the new extension have been in use since September, 1937, so that conductors should now be familiar with them.

WORKMAN TICKETS

Workman tickets will be issued on the new extension on all trolleybuses up to 8.0 a.m. and after this time until arrival at the next farestage point.

GENERAL.

1/- All-day, 6d. All-day Child's and 6d. Tourist (Northern area) tickets will be available over the new extension.

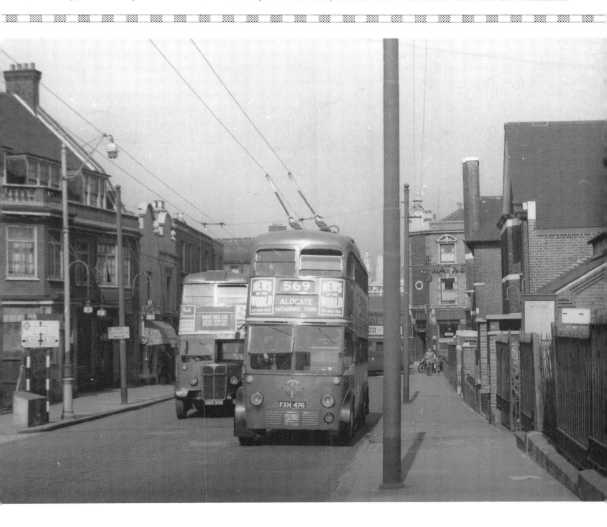

105. The trolleybus route in Albert Road ran next to the railway line serving North Woolwich Station. There is now a fine museum at this location which has displays and exhibits relating to all forms of local transport which once ran in this dockland and industrial area. For the record, the last 669 departed on 2nd February 1960. (C.Carter)

OVERHEAD LAYOUTS

The complexities of trolleybus overhead wiring have always held a fascination. This interest is analogous to the enthusiast's preoccupation with a railway or tramway track layout. On the other hand, it has to be admitted that for many citizens of London, the disappearance of trolleybus wires was welcomed on aesthetic grounds. Whatever the merits of this argument, London Transport did try to produce clean, neat overhead which was well designed and practical. The next few photos show a range of different fixtures and fittings used on routes 696 and 698. After abandonment at the beginning of March 1959, the running wires in the Bexley area were quickly removed, this work being performed mostly at night. The span wires and steel spacer bar hangers had all been cut down by April. Finally, those traction standards not needed by the local authority for street lighting, were uprooted. In the splendid summer of 1959 the author walked from Welling to Crook Log and he noted many holes in the pavement still to be made good by new paving stones. The metal section boxes which supplied power to the overhead, were salvaged one by one, but at least one remained in Welling for many years. The remaining traction standards have also disappeared, the last section of street lighting to employ them was along Bexley Road in Erith. However, this is not the end of the story, as miles of underground cabling were also surplus to requirements; this power supply network was dismantled and some of the below pavement conduits were later re-employed for cable TV and information technology circuits. Thus the old trolleybuses can truly be said to have survived, at least in spirit, into the computer age!

106. Practically all of the double trolley overhead on the LCC Tramways section from Woolwich to Lee Green was hung from span wires attached to traction standards. This unique photo of Eltham High Street shows one of the rare bracket arms installed by the LCC on the 1921 extension from Eltham Church to Lee Green. Ironically, trolleybuses were fated never to run here and local tram services 44, 46 and 72 were replaced by motor buses in July 1952.   (R.J.Harley Coll.)

107. The Griffin Road, Plumstead reverser was installed by LT in 1941 and the lay-by siding on the left of the picture was added towards the end of the war, so that short working trolleys could stand at the stop without interfering with trams and trolleybuses on through services. Reversers were far from ideal and dewirements regularly occurred here; it is interesting to note that only three reversers existed on the vast London system and two thirds of them were encountered in the Woolwich/Dartford area! (J.C.Gillham)

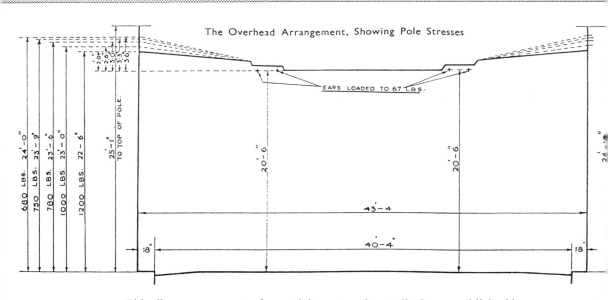

This diagram was part of an article on London trolleybuses published by
Transport World in November 1935

108. On the right hand side of Plumstead High Street is the trailing frog for the junction of routes 696 (from Wickham Lane) and 698 (from Bostall Hill). The facing frog in the top left of this view, was connected to a pull wire attached to a nearby traction standard. This was activated by conductors of 696 trolleybuses which turned right into Wickham Lane. Half way up the standard in the centre of the picture is the indicator box which showed drivers which route their poles were taking. The first standard in Bostall Hill carries a bus stop and is painted with a white band, this warned drivers of a section feed. (J.C.Gillham)

109. A more detailed view of the Villacourt Road junction than in pictures 39 and 40, shows the rather neat arrangement needed for this right angled turn. As many readers may recall, at night the wires used to glisten in the reflection of street lamps and car headlights. (J.C.Gillham)

110. At Knee Hill, Abbey Wood we stop to admire a veritable web of wires. At the top of the picture is a 75 degree crossover with wooden insulation fittings. (B.T.Cooke)

111. The turning circle at Abbey Wood was once the pride and joy of London Transport and in the 1930s guided tours of foreign transport experts would find their way here to admire the artistry. The LT staff magazine "Pennyfare" even featured a view of the layout in its January 1936 edition. The whole set up was eulogised in terms of "steel wires in the sunset." (J.C.Gillham)

ROLLING STOCK

Trolleybus operations in Bexley began with 60 seat Leylands belonging to class B2. They were registered CGF 94-131. Aside from the 16ft. 6ins./5029mm wheelbase Leyland chassis, they had electrical equipment supplied by Metrovick and the bodywork was by Brush. As passenger traffic increased on the Bexley routes, so these vehicles were deemed inadequate and most were transferred elsewhere to make way for larger 70 seat trolleybuses. Although all B2 vehicles had been withdrawn by the early 1950s, the very similar B1 class survived until 1959 working from Sutton Depot (later renamed Carshalton, and described in more detail in companion Middleton Press album *Croydon's Trolleybuses*). Local enthusiast, Peter Moore, spotted Carshalton B1, number 489, working for a few days in the Bexley area whilst several BX vehicles were dried out after the "Storm of the Century" (qv) in September 1958.

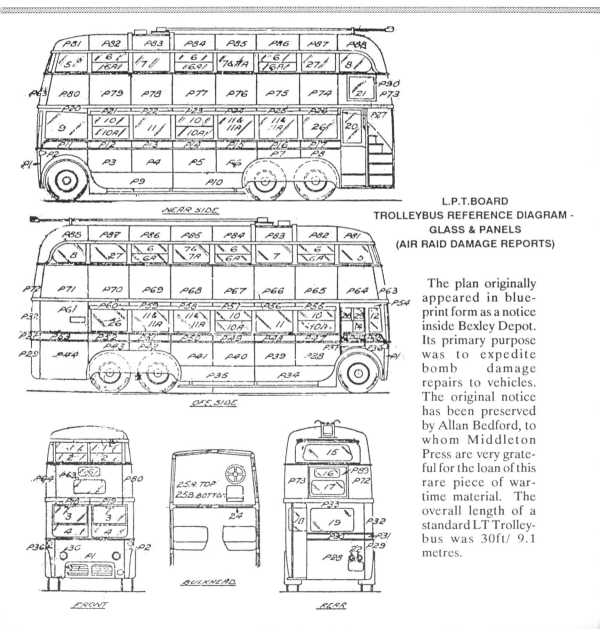

**L.P.T.BOARD
TROLLEYBUS REFERENCE DIAGRAM -
GLASS & PANELS
(AIR RAID DAMAGE REPORTS)**

The plan originally appeared in blueprint form as a notice inside Bexley Depot. Its primary purpose was to expedite bomb damage repairs to vehicles. The original notice has been preserved by Allan Bedford, to whom Middleton Press are very grateful for the loan of this rare piece of wartime material. The overall length of a standard LT Trolleybus was 30ft/ 9.1 metres.

In times of wartime need, other classes of London trolleybuses have made guest appearances on routes 696 and 698, but the bulk of the local fleet eventually consisted of 18ft. 7ins./5664mm wheelbase vehicles of Leyland manufacture belonging to classes D2, D3 and H1. Another characteristic of the latter day fleet was the number of rebodied vehicles which were easily recognised by their more steamlined styling to the front, upper deck window pillars. Suffix-A vehicles were rebodied by Weymann, suffix-B by East Lancashire Coachbuilders, and suffix-C by Northern Coachbuilders.

A modern six-wheel trolley-bus. (1) Slipper picking up current; (2) cable arm; (3) lightning arrester; (4) trolley-bar; (5) air compressor and main light switch; (6) bell and buffer; (7) windscreen wipers; (8) steering wheel; (9) trolley battery change-over switch; (10) control pedal; (11) air brake pedal; (12) bulb horn; (13) hand brake; (14) motor controller and reverser; (15) resistance; (16) inlets for cool air; (17) motor generator sets; (18) air compressor; (19) compressed air reservoir; (20) traction motor; (21) air brake cylinder; (24) rubber front mudguards; (25) ventilators for saloon; (26) scientifically designed seats.

This diagram was published in a 1930s popular science book for students.

112. Brand new number 96 was delivered with a half cab driving compartment. The other half was fitted with a passenger seat, but this proved impractical in operation and all B2 vehicles were later rebuilt with full width driver's cabs. Livery is LT red and cream with black mudguards, silver roof, gold fleet name and numerals.   (LT official photo)

113. This view shows H1 class Leyland, number 798, in immediate post-war condition. The vehicle still has an old style enamel running number on the cream band under the first passenger window next to the driver. Shortly, this would be replaced by bus type aluminium running number and depot code stencils. (C.Carter)

Modifications to Trolleybus Lighting Instructions

In the event of an air raid warning being given during hours of darkness, the driver must switch off the M.G. switch and the headlight, and tell the Conductor to switch on the emergency lights by means of the switch under the staircase. This provides for side and tail lights and a platform light.

On the sixty-seaters operating from Bexley and Holloway the Driver will switch off the M.G. switch and turn the rotary switch in the cabin to the emergency position.

Extract from LT circular, October 1939

This plan appeared in Road Passenger Transport by R.Stuart Pilcher, published in 1937.

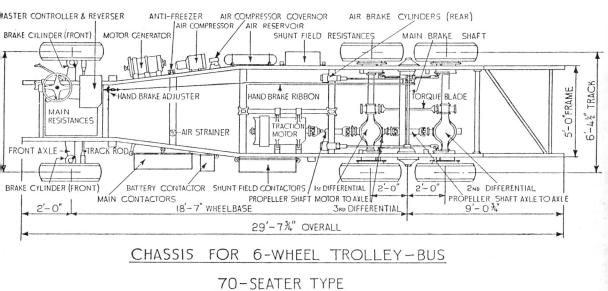

CHASSIS FOR 6-WHEEL TROLLEY-BUS

70-SEATER TYPE

Bexleyheath Trolleybus Depot final wiring layout. Not to scale.

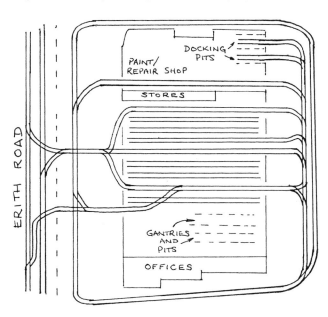

114. A glance at the off-side, rear of D2 class Leyland, number 424, reveals the pleasing design of these vehicles. A dark brown livery was applied to the rear dome surrounding the back window and to most of the roof. The rather attractive paint scheme employed on some of the pre-war trolleys was given up in World War Two, allegedly because the silver roofs made easy to spot targets for low flying German raiders.   (A.B.Cross)

115. A fine view of rebuilt trolley 107A shows the vehicle in pristine condition without advertising on the upper deck side panels. Rebodied by Weymann in 1942, 107A was converted to the longer, standard wheelbase; it was reclassified class D2A. Note the LT TROLLEYBUS transfer above the number plate.   (Lens of Sutton)

Extract from LT circular, January 1943

Destination Blinds—Front and Rear

3127

Bexley Depot

Revised wordings as set out below will shortly be put into service and conductors are asked to note the new arrangement. The present blinds will continue to be used until replacements are required and for a time, therefore, both sets of wording will be in service.

1. PRIVATE
2. PLUMSTEAD
   STATION
3. WICKHAM LN.
   Villacourt Rd.
4. WELLING
   CORNER
5. CRAYFORD
   Princes Rd.
6. { Station Rd.
   { ERITH
   ⌈ via Welling ⌉ 7.
8. { & Bexleyheath ⌋
   ⌊ DARTFORD Mkt. St.
   ⌈ via Welling
9. { & Bexleyheath
   { WOOLWICH FERRY ⌉
   ⌈ Via Erith ⌉ 10.
11. { & Abbey Wood ⌋
    ⌊ BEXLEYHEATH ⌉
    Market Place ⌉ 12.
    via Welling ⌋
13. WORKMAN
14. BEXLEYHEATH
    DEPOT
    ⌈ DARTFORD Mkt. St.
15. { via Erith
    ⌊ & Bexleyheath
16. ABBEY WOOD
    Knee Hill

116. The scene is Penhall Road, Charlton and in the background another victim of the LT tram scrapping mania enters its final resting place. The trolleybus in the foreground is being towed back to Bexleyheath Depot after receiving an overhaul at Charlton Works. In the works themselves there was a short stretch of trolleybus overhead, which was just under two miles away from the nearest wires at Parsons Hill. (C.Carter)

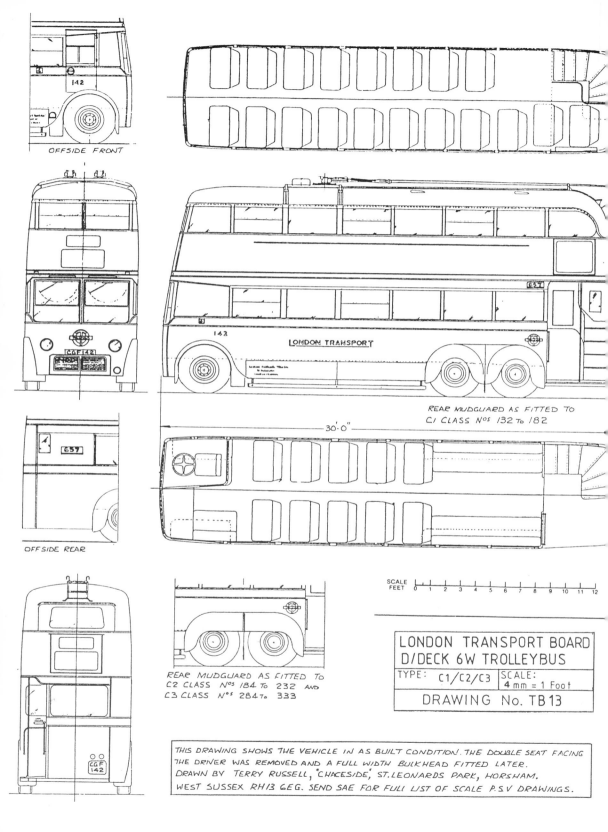

OFFSIDE FRONT

142

OFFSIDE REAR

657

LONDON TRANSPORT

142

CGF 142

657

30'-0"

REAR MUDGUARD AS FITTED TO
C1 CLASS Nᵒˢ 132 To 182

REAR MUDGUARD AS FITTED TO
C2 CLASS Nᵒˢ 184 To 232 AND
C3 CLASS Nᵒˢ 284 To 333

CGF
142

SCALE
FEET 0 1 2 3 4 5 6 7 8 9 10 11 12

LONDON TRANSPORT BOARD D/DECK 6W TROLLEYBUS		
TYPE: C1/C2/C3	SCALE: 4 mm = 1 Foot	
DRAWING No. TB 13		

THIS DRAWING SHOWS THE VEHICLE IN AS BUILT CONDITION. THE DOUBLE SEAT FACING
THE DRIVER WAS REMOVED AND A FULL WIDTH BULKHEAD FITTED LATER.
DRAWN BY TERRY RUSSELL, 'CHASESIDE', ST. LEONARDS PARK, HORSHAM.
WEST SUSSEX RH13 6EG. SEND SAE FOR FULL LIST OF SCALE P.S.V DRAWINGS.

DISASTERS AND DIFFICULTIES

The isolated Bexley routes had their fair share of incidents. As has already been mentioned, the local fleet was almost wiped out by enemy actions in wartime. Aside from man made disasters, the elements took a hand on Friday 5th September 1958, when the (then) "storm of the century" flooded many local roads and caused general chaos. Electricity supplies were also interrupted due to lightning which struck overhead power cables. As the waters rose, so several trolleybuses were caught in the deluge and they sustained damage to their traction motors and electrical equipment. On 6th September, route 696 was worked in two sections either side of the flood waters in Crayford. Vehicles from Dartford either terminated at Princes Road or they executed a battery turn in Crayford Road. It is worth remembering that nearly all London trolleybuses were fitted with traction batteries so that short distances could be negotiated without recourse to overhead wires. Directly after the September inundation, spare trolleybuses were sent over from other depots and these were returned after the mechanical casualties had been "dried out."

Extract from LT circular, July 1937

514.—FLOODS—TROLLEYBUSES.

Trolleybuses must not be driven through floods when the depth of the water is above the bottom edge of the sideward slat. In all cases when driving through floods the speed must not exceed walking pace, and buses should be kept near the crown of the road as possible.

117. And the rains came down! Here in Welling High Street, one wonders what thoughts were going through the driver's mind. With hail stones bouncing all over the trolleybus, it was at least an open question whether he would make it to Dartford and back. (R.J.Harley Coll.)

118. Some problems were easier to sort out, although a dewirement like this one sometimes caused a tail back of other vehicles until the trolleybus got going again. Readers may be intrigued as to the conversation which is about to pass between the driver and the conductress of trolley 369 whilst it is marooned at the junction with Wickham Lane. The topics of "who was driving and at what speed" and "who pulled the frog and when" will be high on the agenda!   (J.C.Gillham)

119. The blast from a German "Doodlebug" caused havoc at the depot. This picture was taken a few hours after the attack on 29th June 1944. (LT official view)

FINALE

120. On 4th March 1959, bus route 229 was extended from Bexleyheath to cover the old 698 to Woolwich. Outside the depot, the triumph of the internal combustion engine seems complete as the condemned trolleys line up ready for the trip to the scrapyard. (L.Rowe)

MP Middleton Press

Easebourne Lane, Midhurst, West Sussex. GU29 9AZ
Tel: 01730 813169 Fax: 01730 812601

Write or telephone for our detailed catalogue of transport, military and local history albums, books and videos

TRAMWAY CLASSICS

Bournemouth & Poole Tramways

Bristol's Tramways

Brighton's Tramways

Camberwell & West Norwood Tramways

Croydon's Tramways

Dover's Tramways

East Ham & West Ham Tramways

Embankment & Waterloo Tramways

Exeter & Taunton Tramways

Greenwich & Dartford Tramways

Hampstead & Highgate Tramways

Hastings Tramways

Ilford & Barking Tramways

Kingston & Wimbledon Tramways

Lewisham & Catford Tramways

Maidstone & Chatham Tramways

North Kent Tramways

Southampton's Tramways

Southend-on-sea Tramways

Southwark & Deptford Tramways

Thanet's Tramways

Victoria & Lambeth Tramways

Walthamstow & Leyton Tramways

Wandsworth & Battersea Tramways

TROLLEYBUS CLASSICS

Croydon's Trolleybuses (published Spring 1996)

Woolwich & Dartford Trolleybuses

LONDON RAILWAY ALBUMS

Clapham Junction to Beckenham Junction

Charing Cross to Orpington

Crystal Palace (High Level) and Catford Loop

Holborn Viaduct to Lewisham

London Bridge to Addiscombe

London Bridge to East Croydon

Mitcham Junction Lines

South London Line

Victoria to Bromley South

West Croydon to Epsom

Waterloo to Windsor

Wimbledon to Epsom